SUPERSTARS OF WRESTLING

Randy Orton

By Ryan Nagelhout

Gareth Stevens
Publishing

RIGHT ON!

Please visit our website, www.garethstevens.com. For a free color catalog of all our high-quality books, call toll free 1-800-542-2595 or fax 1-877-542-2596.

Library of Congress Cataloging-in-Publication Data

Nagelhout, Ryan.
 Randy Orton / Ryan Nagelhout.
    p. cm. — (Superstars of wrestling)
 Includes index.
ISBN 978-1-4339-8532-4 (pbk.)
ISBN 978-1-4339-8533-1 (6-pack)
ISBN 978-1-4339-8531-7 (library binding)
1. Orton, Randy—Juvenile literature. 2. Wrestlers—United States—Biography—Juvenile
literature. I. Title.
 GV1196.O77N35 2013
 796.812092—dc23
 [B]
                                    2012036996

First Edition

Published in 2013 by Gareth Stevens Publishing
111 East 14th Street, Suite 349
New York, NY 10003

Copyright © 2013 Gareth Stevens Publishing

Designer: Nicholas Domiano
Editor: Ryan Nagelhout

Photo credits: Cover background Denis Mironov; cover, pp. 1, 7, 11, 23, 29 Gallo Images/
Getty Images Sport/Getty Images; pp. 5, 13 Bob Levey/WireImage/Getty Images; p. 9 Moses
Robinson/Getty Images Entertainment/Getty Images; pp. 15, 25 Ethan Miller/Getty Images
Entertainment/Getty Images; p. 17 George Koroneos/Shutterstock.com; p. 19 Djamilla Rosa
Cochran/WireImage/Getty Images; p. 21 Don Arnold/WireImage/Getty Images;
p. 27 Ray Mickshaw/WireImage/Getty Images.

Printed in the United States of America

CPSIA compliance information: Batch #CW13GS: For further information contact Gareth Stevens, New York, New York at 1-800-542-2595.

Contents

Meet Randy

Randy Orton is a WWE superstar!

5

Orton was born on April 1, 1980, in Knoxville, Tennessee. He grew up in St. Louis, Missouri.

Orton Tradition

Randy comes from a wrestling family. His grandfather, Bob Orton Sr., and his dad, "Cowboy" Bob Orton, both wrestled. His uncle was a pro, too!

9

Orton started wrestling in 2000 in St. Louis. He signed a contract with the WWE when he was 19!

In 2002, Randy made his WWE debut. He wrestled Hardcore Holly in a match on Smackdown.

Evolution Time

Orton joined the group Evolution with fellow wrestler Triple H. He was picked by many as wrestling's next big thing.

In 2004, Orton won the WWE World Heavyweight Championship. At 24, he was the youngest champion in WWE history!

Killer Moves

Early on, Orton beat many great wrestlers like Mick Foley, Harley Race, Sgt. Slaughter, and "Stone Cold" Steve Austin. He earned himself the nickname "The Legend Killer."

The Viper

Orton wanted to study reptiles, especially snakes, when he was growing up! Later, he became known as "The Viper" for his quick moves in the ring.

In 2007, he won the WWE Championship twice in 1 night! Orton has also won a Tag Team title and the Intercontinental Championship. He also won a Royal Rumble in 2009.

23

Legacy Rule

In 2009, Orton set up his own wrestling group called The Legacy. He asked wrestlers like Cody Rhodes and Ted DiBiase Jr. to join. Their fathers were pro wrestlers, too!

Randy Orton

Cody Rhodes

Orton on Screen

In 2011, Orton hit the silver screen.

He played Ed Freel in the film *That's*

What I Am.

27

What's Next?

Orton's career, in and out of the ring, is just heating up. What will he do next?

29

Timeline

1980   Orton is born on April 1.

2000   Orton first wrestles in pro ranks.

2002   Orton makes his WWE debut.

2004   Orton becomes youngest-ever WWE World Heavyweight champion.

2007   Orton wins WWE Championship twice in 1 night.

2009   Orton wins WWE Royal Rumble.

2011   Orton makes film debut in *That's What I Am*.

For More Information

Books:

Stone, Adam. *Randy Orton*. Minneapolis, MN: Bellwether Media, 2012.

West, Tracey. *Cena & Orton: Rivalry in the Ring*. New York, NY: Grosset & Dunlap, 2011.

Websites:

Online World of Wrestling

onlineworldofwrestling.com/profiles/r/randy-orton.html
Keep track of Randy Orton's matches with this recap.

Randy Orton.com

randy-orton.com/
Look for exclusive photos and information on the official site of Randy Orton.

Publisher's note to educators and parents: Our editors have carefully reviewed these websites to ensure that they are suitable for students. Many websites change frequently, however, and we cannot guarantee that a site's future contents will continue to meet our high standards of quality and educational value. Be advised that students should be closely supervised whenever they access the Internet.

Glossary

champion: a person or team that is the overall winner of a contest or sport

contract: a deal between two parties to work together

debut: a first official public appearance

evolution: the process of change or growth

legacy: something left behind for a person by family

legend: a person or thing that inspires stories

reptile: an animal covered with scales or plates that breathes air, has a backbone, and lays eggs, such as a turtle, snake, lizard, or crocodile

Index